# HIP-HOP
## Biographies

# SEAN COMBS

SADDLEBACK
EDUCATIONAL PUBLISHING

Beyoncé

Chris Brown

**Sean Combs**

Drake

Dr. Dre

50 Cent

Jay Z

Nicki Minaj

Pharrell

Pitbull

Rihanna

Usher

Lil Wayne

Kanye West

SADDLEBACK
EDUCATIONAL PUBLISHING
www.sdlback.com

ISBN-13: 978-1-62250-929-4
ISBN-10: 1-62250-929-3
eBook: 978-1-63078-051-7

Printed in Singapore by Craft Print International Ltd
0000/CA00000000
19 18 17 16 15  1 2 3 4 5

# Table of Contents

# Timeline

**1969:** Sean John Combs is born November 4, 1969, in Harlem.

**1972:** Sean's father, Melvin Combs, is murdered.

**1981:** Combs's mother moves the family to Mount Vernon, New York.

**1988:** Combs goes to Howard University.

**1990:** Combs drops out of school to work at Uptown records.

**1994:** Combs is fired from Uptown Records and starts his own company, Bad Boy Productions.

**1997:** Combs becomes a star with "Can't Nobody Hold Me Down."

**1998:** Combs is nominated for five Grammy Awards and is named rap artist of the year. Combs also starts the Sean John fashion label.

**1999:** His second album, *Forever*, is released. The video "Hate Me Now" creates controversy. Combs is arrested twice that year.

**2000:** Combs produces the TV show *Making the Band*, which features his knack for managing talent and producing music.

**2001:** Combs produces the TV show *Run's House*, starring Reverend Run, a member of Run-DMC, one of Combs's musical heroes. During this year, Combs changes his name from Puff Daddy to P. Diddy. He releases his third album, *The Saga Continues…*

2003: Combs runs in the New York City marathon, raising $2 million for New York City public schools.

2004: Combs appears in the play *A Raisin in the Sun* on Broadway. His fourth album, *We Invented the Remix*, comes out.

2004: Combs wins a menswear designer award from the Council of Fashion Designers of America. He also creates the Vote or Die campaign to encourage young people to vote.

2006: His fifth studio album, *Press Play*, comes out.

2007: Comb's scent, "Unforgivable," wins a Fifi Award.

2010: his sixth studio album, *Last Train to Paris*, is released.

2013: Combs creates Revolt TV, a cable network.

2014: his seventh studio album, *MMM*, is released. That year, Combs speaks to the graduating class at Howard University.

# A Child of Two Worlds

Sean Combs climbed to the top of the music business in record time. As a business person, he went from intern to executive. As a creative person, he started as a producer and also became a performer. Then he tried his hand at fashion. He created a successful clothing business and his own scent. Next he tried acting. Combs is a man of many talents. He is also known by many names: Puffy, Puff Daddy, P. Diddy, and now Diddy.

Combs did not come from a rich family. But he got his drive and style from his parents and grandmother. He strives to be the best at whatever he does. Those qualities helped him succeed. They also helped him overcome his troubles along the way.

Sean John Combs was born on November 4, 1969, in Harlem, New York. His mother, Janice, was a model. She also worked as a teacher. His father, Melvin, drove a taxi. Janice and Melvin wanted to make a good life for Sean and his younger sister, Keisha. It wasn't easy. The family lived in the Esplanade Gardens housing projects.

One day in 1972, everything changed. Sean's father was killed. Sean was only three. Janice told him that Melvin had died in a car accident. Sean learned the truth when he was 14 doing some schoolwork at the library. There, he read the real story of

Sean Combs lived in Harlem until he was 12 years old.

his father's death in a newspaper. Melvin had been a drug dealer, working with Frank Lucas, a famous Harlem gangster. There was no car accident. Melvin had been shot in the head.

Combs never got over the pain of his father's death. He still feels the loss today. He misses being able to share his successes. He misses the opportunity of getting fatherly advice. Now Combs has children of his own—Justin, Jessie James, Christian, Chance, D'Lila, and Quincy. And he wants to be the father he didn't have.

Janice Combs worked hard to send her son to Mount Saint Michael Catholic School.

After Melvin's murder, Janice worked three part-time jobs to support the family. Combs's grandmother helped take care of the children. The two women held the family together. In some ways, Janice had stepped into the role of his father. His grandmother was like a mother.

Janice pushed herself and her children. She wanted to show them a world beyond poverty and crime. When Combs was six years old, Janice hosted a fashion show. Combs was able to flaunt his style on the runway. One summer, Combs went to a Fresh Air Fund camp. He stayed with an Amish family in Pennsylvania.

But meanwhile, Combs needed to survive on the streets of Harlem. Once when he was nine years old, some kids stole his money. He was on his way to the store. He came home in tears. His grandmother hugged him and told it was all right. His mother told him to go back out and get the money. He did. Combs learned to stand up for himself at a young age.

When Combs was 12, Janice moved her children to a safer neighborhood. Janice took them to Mount Vernon, New York. It was not far from Harlem. But it was a world away. There was green grass and Little League. Combs ran two newspaper routes and worked part-time jobs. He had hustle like his dad.

Janice sent her son to a private Catholic school. Tall and fast, he ran track. He also was a defensive back on the football team. The football team won the division championship in 1986. Combs dreamed of playing professionally. In his senior year, that dream died. Combs broke his leg and had to sit out the rest of the season. His leg was broken, but his spirit wasn't. Combs decided to make it in the music business.

Combs often went to Harlem to visit his grandmother. He would sneak out at night to see live concerts in the city. He saw his favorite rappers perform. He saw Run-DMC at Madison Square Garden. He still remembers when Run told everyone to hold up their Adidas. All around, sneakers went up into the air. Combs was impressed by that kind of power.

Combs met famous rappers like Kool Moe Dee. He even performed as a dancer in several music videos. Combs knew that music was his destiny. He dreamed of working at a record label. But Combs did more than dream.

After high school, Combs went to Howard University. It is a black college in Washington, DC. He became popular for throwing large parties. He invited hip-hop artists like Slick Rick to Howard. His friends from that time say he was flashy. He liked be the life of the party. The university could see that Combs was an excellent party promoter. They asked him to plan some of their events.

One event started out great but turned tragic. In 1991, Combs helped organize a celebrity basketball game with a performance by Heavy D. It was a charity event to raise money to fight AIDS. The place was packed, with more people waiting outside. At one point, the people outside crashed through the doors. Nine people died, and more than 20 others were injured.

That night Combs's life turned upside down. He was trying to raise money for a good cause, and now people were dead. People were suing him.

As a teen, Combs was inspired by Run-DMC.

# A Head for Business

Although that event had gone wrong, Combs felt like he was ready to move on to bigger things. He felt like school was getting in his way. He went to New York City to interview for a job. He tried Def Jam Records. He had no luck there, but he didn't give up.

Combs turned to his friend Heavy D for help. Heavy D introduced him to Andre Harrell. Harrell was the founder of Uptown Records. Harrell didn't exactly offer Combs a job. It was an unpaid internship with Uptown. Combs took the position and never looked back.

Combs hadn't put much effort into his college classes. But at Uptown he worked hard to be the best businessman he could be. Combs started out as an assistant. He worked for little to no pay. He got coffee for people and made deliveries. He watched every detail around him. He took notes and learned quickly. Combs was learning the record business on the job.

Combs quickly climbed the ranks at Uptown. He impressed Harrell with his hustle. He was promoted to head of A&R. It was his job to find new talent and shape their image.

In 1991, Combs was assigned to the group Jodeci. He gave them an urban look, dressing them in leather, Timberland boots, jerseys, and sunglasses. Because he didn't have a big budget, Combs had to get creative to market Jodeci. He created a "street team" of teens who passed out flyers and convinced local DJs to play Uptown artists. Jodeci had talent. But Combs made them a success.

Combs got his start at Uptown Records. His friend Heavy D helped him get the job.

When a record *producer* failed to show up one time, Combs stepped into the sound booth. He remixed songs, even though he didn't have any musical training. He said that he just knew how the record should sound. Fans agreed! Combs was promoted again, this time to vice president.

Next, Combs spotted a new artist, Mary J. Blige. He helped her develop her sound. Then Combs produced her *debut* album, *What's the 411?* Like Jodeci, Mary J. Blige was a big success. Her record sold over three million copies. Combs was living his dream.

In only five years, Combs had climbed from intern to vice president. He was the youngest executive in the music industry. The fame went to his head. At this point in his career, he was known as "Puffy."

Combs has kept the story surrounding his nickname a mystery. Many people believe it comes from his time playing football. They say Combs used to puff out his chest to look bigger on the field. Others say he would huff and puff when he was angry as a child. In any case, the name stuck.

It seemed like Combs had the magic touch. But success made him boastful and arrogant around the office. Many of his co-workers found him difficult to work with. Finally, Harrell got tired of the attitude and fired Combs.

Combs was devastated. He had poured everything into his career at Uptown. He had two children and a big, expensive house. What would he do?

Combs discovered his talent for producing records.

15

# Becoming Notorious with Biggie

While at Uptown, Combs had dreamt of having his own company, Bad Boy Entertainment. Bad Boy Entertainment would be more than a record label. It would also be a management firm and a production company. Combs imagined having complete control. He would pick the talent. He would develop it. Then he would record the music.

Combs needed someone to invest money in his dream. He joined forces with Clive Davis. Davis had started Arista Records. Arista was one of the most successful record labels of all time, and that made Davis a very rich man. Davis believed that Combs could be successful. So Davis gave him the money to start Bad Boy.

The first two artists he signed to his new label were Craig Mack and Christopher Wallace (better known as the Notorious B.I.G. or Biggie). Both Mack and Biggie impressed Combs with their raw rhymes about inner-city life.

Mack's single "Flava in Ya Ear" was Bad Boy's first big success. The single went platinum. It was a hit on the hip-hop charts and in the clubs. The remix of that record introduced the Notorious B.I.G. and Busta Rhymes to the hip-hop world. The song is considered a hip-hop classic.

Shortly after Craig Mack's success, Bad Boy Entertainment released *Ready to Die*, the first album by Notorious B.I.G. *Ready to Die* changed hip-hop. Biggie told his stories with a great flair for detail. His raw and gritty voice was unique. He became an instant superstar. *Ready to Die* is considered one of the best rap albums of all time.

Combs's best friend, Biggie, helped make Bad Boy Entertainment a huge success.

As Combs would learn time and again, the road to success was not smooth. In 2006, he was charged with using samples that he did not have permission to use on *Ready to Die.*

Sampling beats had been part of hip-hop from the beginning. The first hip-hop artists, like DJ Kool Herc, freely used beats. They mostly sampled songs from the soul era. But in those days, the hip-hop community was small. And the records didn't make a lot of money. Samples were used without permission. But no one complained.

Then, hip-hop became popular. And records made a lot more money. This changed the way people felt about sampling. They didn't like it when other people made money from their work. So they sued.

After 10 years, the court case against Combs ended. The judge ruled that *Ready to Die* illegally used music that was owned by Bridgeport Music and Westbound Records. The judge said that sales of Biggie's album had to stop. The judge also awarded $4.2 million in fines to Bridgeport Music and Westbound Records. Those court decisions changed the way music is used and shared.

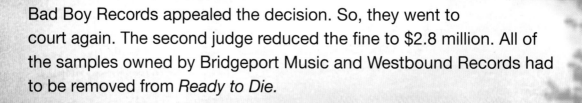

Bad Boy Records appealed the decision. So, they went to court again. The second judge reduced the fine to $2.8 million. All of the samples owned by Bridgeport Music and Westbound Records had to be removed from *Ready to Die.*

The samples used in many of Biggie's songs belonged to other people. This caused a number of court battles.

Combs produced hits for many artists during the 1990s, including Mariah Carey.

Success behind the scenes was not enough for Puff Daddy, as he now called himself. Combs rapped on songs by Bad Boy artists. He sat in a hot tub in the Notorious B.I.G.'s video for "One More Chance." Combs appeared with a long list of music stars such as Aaliyah, TLC, Da Brat, and Queen Latifah in that video. Combs was one of the hottest producers in hip-hop. He was nearly as famous as his stars.

Combs signed the R&B group 112 to Bad Boy. He also signed rapper Ma$e. Then he got to work crafting their hit albums. Folks across the music industry began to recognize Combs's talent. ASCAP (the American Society of Composers, Authors, and Publishers) named Combs Songwriter of the Year for 1996. He produced records by Mary J. Blige, Mariah Carey, and Aretha Franklin. Combs's skills helped create hits for LL Cool J, R. Kelly, and TLC.

Combs had a lot of friends in the business. But Combs and Biggie were especially close. The two were quite a pair. Combs looked downright small and scrawny next to his big and tall friend. But they were good for each other. Combs kept Biggie focused on his career and away from the street. Biggie's skills brought Combs to new heights of success.

Combs had taken Bad Boy from a dream to a company worth millions. He used his eye for talent and his head for business. Bad Boy made Combs a wealthy man. He wanted to use his money to help others. He started Daddy's House Social Programs, a charity for urban kids and their families. But his life was about to take an unexpected turn off easy street.

# Bad Boy vs. Death Row

Combs grew up in New York City where hip-hop was born. Back then, the poor urban neighborhoods looked like a war zone. Empty lots and abandoned buildings were everywhere. Landlords set fire to buildings to collect the insurance money. There were no jobs and lots of crime. Rapping and dancing were art forms that took creativity, not cash. Communities had large block parties, with dancing and DJs.

But in the late 1980s, a new sound starting coming from California. Groups like N.W.A (featuring the young rappers Ice Cube, Dr. Dre, and Eazy E) made gansta rap popular. And in the 1990s, Death Row Records was turning out the platinum hits. Dr. Dre's 1993 solo album *The Chronic* and Snoop Dog's second album, *Doggystyle*, made the sounds of the West Coast fresh and exciting.

Biggie first met West Coast rapper Tupac Shakur on a movie set. Tupac was filming *Poetic Justice* with Janet Jackson. Biggie and Tupac became friends. They recorded a few duets together. They even performed freestyles together at Madison Square Garden. But their friendship didn't last. In 1994, Tupac publically accused Biggie of stealing his rhymes.

Then, a few months later, things between Tupac and the Bad Boy crew would get much worse. One evening in New York, Tupac arrived in the lobby of Quad Recording Studios. He was there to meet Andre Harrell. Harrell was Combs's friend and former boss from Uptown. While waiting for Harrell, Tupac was jumped by two men. They stole his jewelry and shot him multiple times. Combs and Biggie rushed downstairs to see what happened. They got there just as Tupac was being carried away on a stretcher.

A friendly rivalry with Tupac and the other Death Row artists turned unfriendly fast.

Tupac blamed Combs and Biggie for the shooting. The media exploded. *Vibe* magazine interviewed Combs and Biggie. They denied having anything to do with Tupac's shooting. Biggie and Combs said that they considered Tupac a friend. The Bad Boy crew couldn't understand Tupac's beef with them.

A war of words began. Insults were traded back and forth. The beef got bigger. Soon people were talking about East Coast versus West Coast. Radio stations, TV shows, and newspaper articles reported on it. The media was happy to play up the feud. It attracted a bigger audience. Headlines hyped the conflict. It divided fans. And all the talk started to make the feud a reality.

At the Source Awards, Suge Knight called Combs "a showoff." Knight insulted Combs publically on TV. Knight told the rappers to come to Death Row if they wanted a serious producer who didn't dance in their music videos. Ouch! Once again, Combs was being called out for having a big head.

The feud moved from the media to the music. Artists from Bad Boy and Death Row began releasing diss tracks. The attacks got heated. Tupac took Biggie's song "Who Shot Ya?" as a taunt. Tupac fired back with his own diss track. He aimed "Hit 'Em Up" at Biggie.

Death Row released a video for "New York, New York." In it, West Coast rappers appeared as giants. They stomped on Brooklyn like Godzilla. East Coast rappers followed-up with a video for "LA, LA." In that video, Bad Boy rappers threw body bags of West Coast rappers off the Brooklyn Bridge. The images were getting more violent. The line between art and threat was not clear.

East Coast rappers Havoc and Prodigy of Mobb Deep, along with Capone-N-Noreaga and Tragedy Khadafi, responded to Death Row's diss with "LA, LA."

On September 7, 1996, Tupac went to see Mike Tyson fight in Las Vegas. After the fight, he got into a car heading to a club. Another car pulled up beside Tupac. And a gunman shot Tupac through the window. No one knew if Tupac would survive. He was rushed to the hospital.

A bullet had punctured Tupac's lung. He suffered internal bleeding. He couldn't breathe without the help of machines. After six days in the hospital, Tupac died. The hip-hop community mourned the loss of this talented star. Tupac Shakur was only 25 years old.

Early in the morning on March 9, 1997, it was six months after Tupac's murder. Biggie was in a car leaving a *Vibe* party in Los Angeles with Combs and other Bad Boy members. An SUV pulled up beside the car. Biggie was shot four times in the chest. He died before reaching the hospital. He was only 24.

The two murders were very similar. Rumors spread like wildfire. Were the police involved? Were gang members to blame? Were the murders caused by the East Coast-West Coast feud? People had a lot questions that remain unanswered. Both cases are open and unsolved to this day.

In New York, the hip-hop community mourned the loss of Biggie. Thousands of fans lined the streets to watch his funeral *procession*. Limos with flowers that spelled "B.I.G." rode slowly to the funeral home. Fans showed their appreciation. They chanted his name and held signs. They blasted his music through the streets.

Biggie's funeral in Brooklyn brought people out in the streets to mourn together.

Combs went from a supporting role to leading man. His first album was a huge hit.

# Bouncing Back

Biggie's death hit Combs hard. On the day of the funeral, Combs had to face one of the hardest tasks of his life. He had to give a eulogy for his best friend. He spoke from his heart. But the grief remained. Combs struggled to move past his sadness.

Combs spoke with Biggie's family about releasing Biggie's next album. They decided to go forward with it. Two weeks after Biggie's death, Bad Boy Records released *Life After Death*. The title is eerie. It was recorded months before Biggie's murder. Biggie rapped about his death in the lyrics of several songs. The album cover featured Biggie posing next to a hearse. It is no wonder Combs found it difficult to release the music of his late friend.

*Life After Death* made hip-hop history. The album debuted at number one. It went diamond. That means it was a platinum record 10 times over. The album secured Biggie's spot in the hip-hop record books. It is considered one of the best rap albums of all time.

Combs distracted himself by working on his own material. On July 1, 1997, he dropped his first album, *No Way Out*. His first single was "Can't Nobody Hold Me Down." It was a massive hit. And the hits kept coming. There was "Victory," "Been Around the World," and "It's All About the Benjamins." Combs was nominated for five Grammy Awards. He won for best rap album in 1998.

The standout single on *No Way Out* was called "I'll Be Missing You." It was a star-studded tribute to the Notorious B.I.G. It sampled a hit song by the Police called "Every Breath You Take." Combs was finished with tough talk and threats. He showed a softer, caring side. This modeled a different kind of manhood for the hip-hop audience. "Words can't express what you mean to me," Combs rapped. Biggie's widow, Faith Evans, and the group 112 sang the hook.

The song played on radios and TVs across the nation. Anyone who had ever lost a loved one could relate. However, "I'll Be Missing You" spoke directly to the community that was still losing too many young men to street violence. And that song stayed at the top of the charts for weeks.

The album *No Way Out* appealed to a wide audience. It won Combs many new fans. His music crossed boundaries. "It's All About the Benjamins" featured guitar licks by rocker Dave Grohl (of the bands Nirvana and the Foo Fighters). Combs became one of the most successful crossover artists in hip-hop.

Combs did not just work on rap albums. He produced Mariah Carey's mega-hit songs "Fantasy" and "Honey." He also produced Jennifer Lopez's first album, *On the Six*. Combs's hits had a unique sound. He mixed soul, pop, rock, and hip-hop. Combs brought a funky new sound to the airwaves.

Puff Daddy became a household name. And with all that fame and money came flashy clothes and expensive bling. Combs loved to show off his hard-earned wealth. He was creating more than hit records now. He was creating a lifestyle.

Once Combs found his voice, he had a lot to say.

Combs's unofficial motto was "Go big or go home." In 1997, he put on the "No Way Out" tour. The tour was unlike any other in hip-hop history. It was like an all-star tour. It featured superstars like Jay Z, Busta Rhymes, Lil' Kim, Nas, and Usher. The tour earned nearly $15 million. It was the most successful hip-hop tour to date. These artists came together for the "No Way Out" tour to symbolize an end to violence within the hip-hop community. The rappers were tired of feuding. They were ready for harmony.

Combs started to make his videos like mini-movies. In the video for Biggie's "Hypnotize," Combs and Biggie escape from the law. There is a suspenseful chase. Helicopters swoop in on a party on Biggie's and Combs's yacht. They interrupt the party. The rappers escape to an underwater party filled with mermaids. It had lots of action. Street reality was replaced with Hollywood fantasy. The rappers appeared like James Bond-type heroes or CEOs.

Combs was a successful man now. His style was a lot more Gatsby than gangster. Jay Gatsby is a fictional character in a novel called *The Great Gatsby* by F. Scott Fitzgerald. The character Gatsby lives in a fabulous mansion and throws over-the-top parties. Gatsby has "new money." That means that Gatsby didn't grow up with money and fancy manners. He didn't inherit the money, he earned it himself. That made him an outsider in a world of "old money." This was a character that Combs could relate to. In fact, Combs started throwing fancy parties of his own in 1998. All kinds of celebrities attended. Everyone wore white. A reporter once asked Combs if he had read *The Great Gatsby.* Combs answered, "Have I read *The Great Gatsby*? I *am* the Great Gatsby."

Combs was expanding the image of rappers by showing the extravagant lifestyle that he and his family maintained.

Combs had always loved fashion. He took after his mother in that way. He styled and shaped the image of stars, such as Jodeci and Mary J. Blige. And he dressed to impress in crisp suits and ties.

Combs wanted to try the fashion business. He founded the popular fashion line Sean John. Sean John made clothes for urban customers with a taste for the finer things. Designers had been borrowing from hip-hop fashion for years. Hip-hop stars and their fans wore brands such as Tommy Hilfiger, Nautica, and Polo Ralph Lauren. Combs decided that the hip-hop community should make its own fashion.

Sean John clothes have been selling well for over a decade. The company earns a reported $525 million each year. Combs has had a lot of firsts with his fashion line. He created the first African American business to open on Fifth Avenue in New York City. In 2001, Combs produced the first nationally televised runway show from Fashion Week. His Sean John collection was broadcast on E! Television and the Style Network. In 2004, Sean John won an award from the Council of Fashion Designers of America (CFDA). He was Menswear Designer of the Year. He became the first African American man to win that important award.

Combs introduced fragrances to Sean John. His scent "Unforgivable" quickly became a number-one seller. Again, Combs made history becoming the first African American to win the fragrance industry's annual Fifi Award.

Sean John fashions, advertised here in New York City's Times Square, became as successful as his music.

# Mo' Money Mo' Problems

One of the hit singles from Biggie's *Life After Death* is "Mo' Money Mo' Problems." On that track, Combs and Biggie rapped about experiencing trouble despite their fame. The rappers warned listeners that making money doesn't always make life easier. Combs would soon find out just how true those words were.

While Combs's fashion line rocketed to success, Bad Boy slowly declined. By 1999, the hits came less frequently. Album sales slowed. Combs's second album, *Forever*, received mixed reviews. Artists began to leave the label. Even worse, Faith Evans accused Combs of keeping the royalties from her hit songs. Combs turned to Andre Harrell, his former boss from Uptown. Harrell managed the struggling Bad Boy label for Combs.

That same year, Combs's relationship with actress and pop star Jennifer Lopez went public. Paparazzi followed them around. Combs and J Lo made news headlines wherever they went. They were hip-hop's power couple. The relationship lasted two years.

Not everyone wished the couple well. Combs had recently fathered a baby with longtime girlfriend Kim Porter. Media gossips complained that Combs had moved on too quickly. They said that Combs had abandoned Porter for Lopez.

But Lopez was only one complication in Combs's personal life. Combs had his eldest son, Justin, in 1993 with his first girlfriend, Misa. He had his second son, Christian, in 1998 with Kim, his on-again, off-again girlfriend. He also took on the role of stepfather to Quincy, Kim's son from another relationship. In 2006, he had his oldest daughter, Chance, with Sarah, a woman he was seeing at the same time as Kim. And five months after Chance was born, Kim gave birth to twin girls, D'Lila Star and Jessie James. Combs has tried to stay on good terms with all of his children's mothers over the years.

Combs's relationship with Jennifer Lopez was followed closely by the press.

Combs's relationship with Lopez was not the only thing in Combs's life making news in 1999. Combs had been working with Nas on the track "Hate Me Now." Nas and Combs put powerful religious images in their video. They wore crowns of thorns on their heads. They carried crosses on their shoulders. The controversial video ended with both rappers up on crosses.

Combs couldn't decide if he should show the "Hate Me Now" video to the world. He had carefully created an image of himself as a successful businessman and a caring father. He had left the street life far behind. Because of this, critics said he had gone soft and sold out. The video was bold enough to prove the critics wrong. It would shock people. But his experience at Catholic school caused him to hesitate. He wondered about his responsibility as a public figure. Did the video go too far? Combs spoke to his priest about it. In the end, Combs decided to edit the video. He cut the most offensive scene.

But something went wrong. The original video, not the edited version, was shown on MTV. Protests immediately sprang up. Many people were upset by the video. They thought it was disrespectful.

Once Combs learned about the mistake, he could not control his anger. He rushed to the office of Nas's manager, Steve Stoute. Combs smashed a champagne bottle into Stoute's head. In a moment of blind rage, Combs had slipped back into the rough ways of his Harlem youth. He was charged with assault. He also had to pay money to Stoute for pain and suffering.

Combs and Nas made a video together for the song "Hate Me Now." But the wrong version got released.

39

# From Puffy to Diddy

For Combs, 1999 had not been an easy year. And it wasn't over yet. The day after Christmas, Combs went to a New York nightclub with Jennifer Lopez. They had a large *entourage* with them. At around 2:30 a.m., Combs and his group got into a brawl. Gunshots rang out. People in the club scattered in fear.

Luckily, no one was killed. But three people were injured. Police interviewed witnesses. The witnesses claimed that Combs and Shyne were both carrying guns. Shyne was the latest rapper that Combs had been promoting. Combs, his bodyguard, Shyne, and Lopez were all arrested when police found a gun in their SUV. Lopez was released with no *charges* against her. Combs, his bodyguard, and Shyne faced charges. There was a possibility that Combs would have to serve jail time.

Combs hired a team of high-powered lawyers. He was eventually cleared of all criminal charges. The case was dropped. Combs was free. He was also single. Combs and Lopez broke up shortly after the arrest.

Comb's bodyguard was cleared of all charges too. But Shyne was found guilty. He was sentenced to 10 years in prison for assault. Shyne was dropped by Bad Boy while in prison. The promising rapper whose talent had been compared to the Notorious B.I.G. was forgotten.

Combs was tired of his bad boy reputation. He was ready to turn the page.

Combs's legal troubles caused him to evaluate his life. Was he a respectable businessman and role model? Or was he a bad boy for life? Combs made his decision and did not look back.

The year 2000 rang in a new millennium. It was time for a change. And in 2001, Combs renamed himself P. Diddy. He wanted to signal that he was leaving his bad boy image behind. The name "Puff Daddy" had to go.

While still producing music and managing his clothing line, Combs produced two hit TV reality shows. The first was called *Making the Band*. It centered around Combs creating and managing different urban singing groups. A few years later, he produced another show. This one was called *Run's House*. It was a reality show about Reverend Run, the former rapper from the group Run-DMC It was hard to believe. Combs was producing a TV show about the rapper who had inspired him as a teen!

Next, Combs tried his hand at acting and succeeded at that too. His acting credits include the movies *Made* (2001), *Monster's Ball* (2001), and *Carlito's Way* (2005). In 2004, Combs took on Broadway. He played Walter Lee in the play *A Raisin in the Sun*. People were surprised by Combs's talent. He was so good that he played the role again in the 2008 TV movie. He won an NAACP (National Association for the Advancement of Colored People) Award for his role.

But Combs wasn't finished surprising his fans. He ran the New York City Marathon in 2003. Although he didn't have much time to train and had a sore knee, Combs finished the race. He completed the 26.2 miles in four hours and 15 minutes. His effort raised $2 million for New York City public schools.

Combs took on the New York City Marathon to raise money for New York City public schools.

Combs gave a speech to students graduating from Howard University. He told them what he learned and why he wished he hadn't dropped out.

In 2005, Combs decided to go by the name Diddy. He dropped the P. Although his name was shorter, his empire continued to grow. Most recently, Combs *founded* Revolt. It is a digital cable TV network that connects young people through music.

Combs spends a lot of his energy on young people. In 2004, he founded the organization Citizen Change. He wanted to inspire young people to vote. Combs went on a nationwide campaign. He used the phrase "Vote or Die" to stress the importance of voting. Combs was one of the first hip-hop *moguls* to get into politics.

Combs also supports worthy causes like AIDS research, childhood diabetes, and education. He remembers what it was like to grow up in Harlem. And he wants to create opportunities for kids. He wants them to have a chance to succeed. He doesn't want them to end up hustling on the streets like his dad.

In 2014, Combs was asked to speak to the graduating students at Howard University. He spoke to them honestly. He spoke about the *consequences* of dropping out of school. College could have taught him to make better business deals. And he might have learned to write better. He said that he had had to learn many things the hard way.

No one knows what Combs might try next. He has gone from one success to another. It's true that Combs has experienced some major setbacks along the way. But he never gives up. He learns from each experience. Each struggle has given him an opportunity to become a better man. And Combs knows how to handle opportunity.

# Vocabulary

| | | |
|---|---|---|
| A&R | (noun) | a department in a record company. A&R stands for "Artists and Repertoire." The A&R people are responsible for finding talent and keeping them popular. |
| acting credit | (noun) | a list of acting jobs |
| airwaves | (noun) | the sound put out by radio stations |
| Amish | (adjective) | referring to the Amish, a group of religious people who live simply, without electricity |
| beef | (noun) | an argument |
| broadcast | (verb) | to show on TV |
| charge | (noun) | a crime that a person is accused of after being arrested |
| consequences | (noun) | the negative results of an action |
| controversial | (adjective) | likely to start an argument |
| craft | (verb) | to make something with care |
| crossover | (adjective) | popular with more than one kind of audience, such as hip-hop and pop |
| debut | (adjective) | first, introduced into the world for the first time |
| diss tracks | (noun) | songs that are meant to insult someone |
| eerie | (adjective) | strange and a little creepy |
| entourage | (noun) | a group of people who travel with a celebrity as friends or workers |
| eulogy | (noun) | a speech that is given at funeral to honor the person who has just died |
| freestyles | (noun) | raps that are made up on stage, not written in advance |
| found | (verb) | to start a business or other organization |
| Godzilla | (noun) | a giant lizard monster from old movies |
| hearse | (noun) | a special kind of car used for funerals |

| | | |
|---|---|---|
| hesitate | (verb) | to take some time before acting or deciding because you are not sure |
| hook | (noun) | a catchy tune or beat that helps makes a song easy to remember |
| hustle | (noun) | the quality of working hard and showing effort |
| hype | (verb) | to exaggerate |
| insurance money | (noun) | money that you get back from an insurance company when something happens to the property that you had paid money to protect |
| intern | (noun) | a job that is taken for the experience since there is little or no pay |
| internal bleeding | (noun) | bleeding inside your body |
| invest | (verb) | to give money to a business or a project in order to make even more money than you started with |
| lot | (noun) | a piece of land for building on |
| mogul | (noun) | a very successful business man |
| paparazzi | (noun) | photographers who take pictures of celebrities for a living |
| party promoter | (noun) | someone who organizes and advertises large parties |
| platinum | (adjective) | selling at least a million copies |
| procession | (noun) | like a parade but for a serious occasion |
| producer | (noun) | someone who is responsible for how a recording sounds |
| samples | (noun) | pieces of music that come from other songs |
| star-studded | (adjective) | filled with stars |
| sue | (verb) | to take someone to court in order to make them pay money you believe they owe you |
| symbolize | (verb) | to show something without saying it directly |

# Photo Credits